The First Voyage Around the World

EXPLORATION AND DISCOVERY

EXPLORATION AND DISCOVERY

The First Voyage Around the World

The story of Ferdinand Magellan's three-year journey through South America and the Pacific Ocean

David White

Mason Crest Publishers
Philadelphia

Mason Crest Publishers
370 Reed Road
Broomall PA 19008

Mason Crest Publishers' world wide web address is
www.masoncrest.com

First printing

1 3 5 7 9 8 6 4 2

Library of Congress Cataloging-in-Publication Data
on file at the Library of Congress

ISBN 1-59084-054-2

Contents

Into the Unknown

THEY HAD THOUGHT it would take three or four days. That was 98 days ago. The once-proud ships of Ferdinand Magellan were now in danger of falling apart and sinking. The once-happy crews were starving and thirsty. They wanted to turn back now more than ever. As far as they could see in every direction, there was only water.

The voyage had left Spain in 1519 with five ships and about 280 Spanish sailors. They were on a mission to the Moluccas, a group of islands in the Far East that were also called the Spice Islands. They were to bring back *spices* from these islands to sell in Spain and other European countries.

8 The First Voyage Around the World

Magellan was hoping to succeed where Christopher Columbus had failed nearly 30 years earlier. Columbus had tried to reach the Far East by sailing west across the Atlantic Ocean. His way had been blocked by large continents that had been unknown to Europeans—North and South America.

Magellan had convinced the king of Spain that he knew about a water passage through South America. The king gave Magellan enough money to buy and equip five ships. These ships then sailed across the Atlantic Ocean and down the east coast of South America. After many months of searching, they found the **strait**. It was later called the Strait of Magellan. The passage was rough, but the ships made it through. On the other side was a giant body of water.

Maps of the time showed the Spice Islands to be just on the other side of South America. Once the ships reached the western side of South America, Magellan thought, it would be just a few more days until they reached their goal. He was dead wrong.

When the sailors entered this body of water, they marveled at how calm it was. Magellan named it the Pacific ("Peaceful") Ocean. In some places, it proved to be too peaceful. Ships at that time were powered by sails. Without wind, the sails wouldn't move. More than once, the ships came to a dead halt in the middle of nowhere. Wind came to be a welcome friend.

The explorers had gotten food and water everywhere they had stopped, but it just wasn't enough. Men were dying. Many had **scurvy**, a disease that sailors got when they didn't get enough vitamins. Those who survived were eating biscuit powder and leather. Their supply of fresh water had long since run out.

Finally, on March 6, 1521, Magellan and his crew landed on the island of Guam. This was a major port with a large population. Never had fresh food looked so good. Never had fresh water tasted so fine. Never had sleep and rest been more welcome. The sailors took their fill of fresh food and water and then slept for many hours.

They had crossed the vast Pacific Ocean.

FERDINAN · MAGELLANVS · SVPERATIS
ANTARCTICI · FRETI · ANGVSTIIS · CLARISS

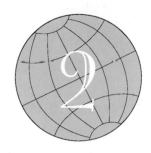

The Formation of an Idea

THE COMMANDER of the first voyage around the world was an experienced sailor named Ferdinand Magellan. He had been born in 1480 in northern Portugal, a small country on the coast of Europe that had a rich seafaring tradition.

Very little is known about Ferdinand Magellan's early life. His parents did not have a lot of money, but they had important friends. It was through these friends that they got young Ferdinand a position at the court of the queen of Portugal.

While at the royal court, Ferdinand saw many important people. He may very well have seen Christopher Columbus,

Ferdinand Magellan is the English version of the explorer's name. His Portuguese name is Fernão de Magalhães.

who stopped at Lisbon on his return journey to Spain after landing in the New World in 1492. Columbus landed in Portugal because of bad weather. While there, he visited the king and queen. The Portuguese explorer Vasco da Gama also visited the court after returning from India in 1499. Gama was the first European to sail around the southern tip of Africa and make it all the way to India. Meeting these explorers may have inspired Magellan to explore the unknown himself.

All of the contacts Magellan made while at court helped shape his view of the world and the people in it. The more he heard about voyages to the east, the more he wanted to go. In 1505, when Magellan was 25 years old, he joined Portugal's navy.

Magellan shipped out shortly after that on a voyage to India. He soon found out, however, that life at sea was not always as exciting as he had thought. He was used to living in nice quarters and wearing nice clothes. He was used to eating good food and sleeping in a warm bed. On a ship at sea, he had none of this. The food that sailors took with them was limited. Ships would often have to stop and buy more food as they went. The sailors slept below deck. When

Portugal began exploring the Atlantic under the direction of Prince Henry the Navigator, a 15-century nobleman who financed many voyages. His goal was finding a sea route around Africa to Asia. Portugal finally accomplished this goal in 1499, nearly 40 years after Prince Henry's death.

the waves rolled high against the ship, water crept into the sailors' quarters. Magellan probably slept on a wet bed most of the time. The promise of India, however, helped Magellan endure these rough conditions.

The ships stopped at various ports along the way. Magellan and the others met Africans and Asians and saw the spices and other goods these people had. All these things would help Magellan decide later on that he wanted to return to the East.

The king of Portugal also wanted his sailors to build forts in India and other areas of the East. These would be used as

Vasco da Gama

Vasco da Gama (1469–1524) was born in Sines, Portugal. As son of the town's governor, he was educated as a nobleman and eventually served in the court of King John II. He also was a naval officer. In 1492, he successfully defended Portuguese colonies on the coast of Guinea from attacks by the French.

Gama's contemporaries viewed him as a ruthless man and a cruel taskmaster. In 1495, he was given command of an expedition to reach India by sea. Some historians claim the task had been given to his brother, Estavao, but that Estavao died before the mission began. Others claim the job was first offered to Gama's other brother, Paolo, who turned it down. This claim seems unlikely, since Paolo accompanied Gama on the expedition.

When Gama returned from his voyage to India, he and the members of his crew were greeted as heroes. Gama made a second voyage to India four years later, where he made trading arrangements with the rulers of major cities and set up the first Portuguese trading posts. In 1524 the king placed Gama in charge of India. Gama died later that year.

trading posts, so that valuable goods could be shipped back to Portugal. They would also be bases from which the Portuguese could spread their religion, Christianity, among the people of the East. Most of these people practiced other religions, such as Islam, Hinduism, or Buddhism. Many battles were fought over religious beliefs.

During his first voyage, Magellan was personally involved in two battles with the natives. In one, he saved the lives of many members of the crew.

The Portuguese ships had stopped to buy food and water, and many of the natives had come on board to see a European ship. Most of the sailors were on land at the time. The natives on board the ships suddenly started attacking

This model shows a popular Portuguese sailing ship, the caravel. Developed by Prince Henry the Navigator, caravels were sturdy ships used by many explorers, including Magellan.

the remaining sailors. Magellan had remained on board one
of the ships and had warned the captain about the possibil-
ity of an attack. The captain was not surprised, therefore,
when the attack came. However, the sailors were outnum-

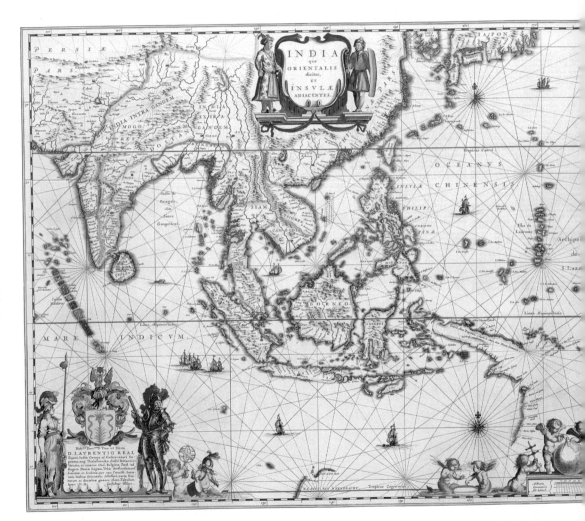

**This map from the early 17th century shows India and the islands
called the East Indies. When Magellan was a young man, Portugal
was attempting to establish control over trade in the Indian
Ocean. When he was 25, Magellan joined the Portuguese navy. Over
the next seven years, he had many adventures.**

bered. At the first sign of trouble, the sailors on land tried to fight their way back to their ships. Magellan and a small band of sailors paddled a small boat ashore, to help their fellow sailors get off the beach and back to the ships. The sailors fought hard enough to end the attack, but about a quarter of them died that day.

The purpose of the voyage to India was to bring back spices and other goods, to build forts, and to spread the Christian religion. Magellan agreed with all of these motives, and they would have a huge effect on him in years to come.

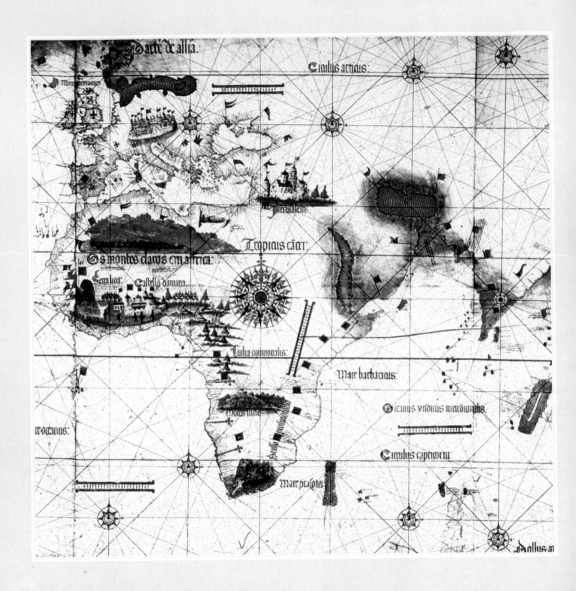

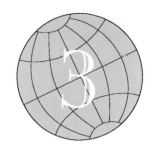

Rejected by the King

PORTUGAL IN THE 1500s was a wealthy country. Its voyages around the tip of Africa and to India and beyond were bringing in a tremendous amount of money. These voyages brought in goods that Portuguese merchants could sell in their own country and in other countries. It was a good time to live in Portugal.

By 1507, Magellan had become an experienced sailor, and was made captain of his own ship. The Portuguese navy was fighting against Arabs over control of the Indian Ocean. Magellan was wounded during one encounter. He also took part in important battles at Goa in 1510 and Malacca in 1511. These victories helped Portugal gain control of the region. By controlling the Strait of Malacca, the Portuguese could control all trade through Malaysia. They could protect their own ships from attack, and they could also keep ships from other countries from returning home with their goods.

The success of the Portuguese navy added to Magellan's reputation. When he returned to Lisbon, the capital of Portugal, in 1512, most of the people at the Portuguese court knew who he was. He also had the respect of those in the navy.

Feeling successful and supported, Magellan confidently asked the king for an increase in his pay when he visited him in Lisbon. Magellan saw others at court who had done much less than he had, yet were paid much more than he was. He thought he should be earning what he was worth.

Perhaps Magellan should have tried to flatter the king first. A few weeks earlier, Magellan had been accused of *deserting* his military post in Morocco. Although the charge was false, and Magellan had been proven innocent, the king was suspicious of the tough sailor. Even after Magellan gave the king papers proving that he was innocent, the king was wary and did not trust Magellan.

> **Magellan was seriously wounded during a battle in 1508. He would walk with a limp for the rest of his life.**

الفـــرآن ثم ونبعد اسـاطير بلاها ورخارف جلالها وقال اركبوا بها بسـم الله مجراها
ومرساها ثم نفش نفش المعسبنر او عباد الله المكرمين وقال اما انا

This drawing from a 14th-century Arab book shows a *dhow*, a vessel commonly used by Arabs in the Indian Ocean. The ships were easy to maneuver because of their triangular sails—an innovation the Portuguese explorers soon adopted for their own ships. When Magellan arrived with the Portuguese fleet, he soon found himself in charge of a small ship and instructed to sink Arab *dhows*. Magellan took part in the fighting in the East from 1505 to 1512.

Rejected by Portugal, Magellan traveled to Spain, where he had friends who would help him. An audience with King Charles V was arranged, and Magellan convinced the ruler that he could succeed where Columbus had failed by leading a voyage west across the Atlantic, finding a route through the Americas, and reaching the Far East.

Have Money, Will Sail

MAGELLAN'S SUCCESSES AS a sailor and leader in the Portuguese navy in India gave him experience and confidence. He had also learned a new way to navigate at sea: *celestial navigation*.

For years, sailors had kept their ships within sight of land because they didn't want to get lost. During the 15th century, astronomers found a way to look at the stars in the night sky and use that information to tell where they were on the Earth. This worked on land, and it worked at sea. This was a wonderful advancement for sailors. They could sail directly across seas or oceans without having to keep the coastline in sight. Celestial navigation helped Columbus

The goal of Christopher Columbus's 1492 voyage was to sail west across the Atlantic Ocean to reach China and the Indies. When he set out from Spain, however, Columbus had not realized that an enormous landmass blocked his way. Columbus made four voyages to the Americas, but never understood that he had arrived at new lands rather than in the Far East. By Magellan's time, however, it was understood that the Americas were continents that most Europeans had not known about.

arrive safely in the New World. Magellan wanted to use the new technique, also.

Magellan had served on many ships while in Portugal's navy, and he had seen up close what was needed to captain a ship. He soon became convinced that he could lead his own voyage of discovery.

Magellan's friend Francisco Serrão had served with him in

> Magellan chose the Spice Islands as his goal for the voyage. These are the Moluccas, in what is now Indonesia. Nutmeg and cloves were two of the many spices to be found there. These spices were very valuable in Europe at the time because they were hard to get

the Indian Ocean. When the Portuguese ships reached the Moluccas, or Spice Islands, Serrão decided to stay. This is part of the reason why Magellan wanted to return to these islands. He wanted to see his friend again. Also, he still wanted to find a shorter route. The Portuguese route to the east—south around the tip of Africa, then northeast to India and the Spice Islands—was about 14,000 miles.

Christopher Columbus' success in sailing west had made other explorers want to do the same. As more people landed in the New World, they realized how large it was. In the early 1500s, Portugal's Pedro Cabral discovered Brazil. In 1513, the Spanish conquistador Vasco Núñez de Balboa crossed the *isthmus* of Panama and became the first

> When Vasco Núñez de Balboa crossed Panama, he named the large body of water he found there the South Sea, because he had traveled south across the isthmus. Magellan himself would later name the vast body of water the Pacific, because he thought it was more peaceful than the Atlantic Ocean.

European to see the Pacific Ocean.

Explorers were also trying to find a way through the lands to the Far East. Magellan thought he could find a strait through the vast continent known as South America. A sailor named Juan Diaz de Solis had reached South America in 1516 and reported a waterway that went west as far as the eye could see. He couldn't sail through this waterway because of bad weather, however, so he turned around and headed home.

Seeking support for his idea, Magellan traveled to Spain, Portugal's rival. In Spain, he found a powerful friend, a man named Diogo Barbosa. Barbosa was interested in exploration. He wanted to get to the East, too. He had many important friends, and he had a lot of money. Barbosa helped Magellan's idea become a reality.

Magellan also made a friend at the Office of Trade and Commerce. This man's name was Juan de Aranda, and he helped Magellan get an audience with the king.

King Charles of Spain was interested in Magellan's idea,

Diogo Barbosa

Diogo Barbosa was a Spaniard who had a lot of power and a lot of money. He liked Ferdinand Magellan so much that he invited him to live with his family. Barbosa had four sons and a daughter. His oldest son, Duarte, was an experienced sailor. He had been on a few voyages to India and the East. Diogo Barbosa encouraged Magellan to get to know his daughter, Beatriz. They were married in 1517.

Barbosa was instrumental in helping Magellan get an appointment to see King Charles of Spain. When Magellan's voyage was approved, Barbosa helped purchase supplies for the five ships. He also allowed his son Duarte to serve aboard the *Trinidad*, which was captained by Magellan himself.

especially the idea of finding a secret passage. Magellan claimed to know exactly where to go to sail through South America and on to the East. The king wanted to claim some of the lands in the East for Spain. He wanted his country to keep up with Portugal, which had already claimed many lands in the East, including much of India. Soon, Captain-General Magellan was in charge of getting ships and crews ready. The king gave him five ships and enough money to buy supplies and pay crewmembers.

Getting ready for the voyage seemed to take forever. Magellan had to buy enough food and water for a long voy-

This 19th-century illustration shows Magellan's coat-of-arms. His signature, taken from old papers in the archives of Portugal, is reproduced at the bottom.

age. He had to find enough men to serve on all those ships. He also had to make sure the ships were prepared to sail a long time.

A man named Sebastian Alvarez, however, was doing all he could to ruin Magellan's plans. Alvarez had been sent by King Manuel of Portugal. Manuel still didn't like Magellan and didn't want Spain to get all the glory of finding a westward sea passage to the Indies. However, King Manuel did not want to make his fellow king mad. So he secretly sent Alvarez to stir up trouble. Supplies got lost, boats sprung leaks, and crewmen were in bad moods. Once, Magellan was almost arrested simply for flying his own flag aboard his ship. Alvarez told anyone who would listen that Magellan's ships were not seaworthy. Many men decided not to join the voyage after all. As a result, the sailors who did sign on to sail with Magellan were not the best sailors around.

Magellan also had a family to worry about. He had been married two years before all this began, and he had a six-month-old son. When the voyage began, Magellan's wife was pregnant again.

Magellan worked long and hard, however, and the ships were finally ready. On September 20, 1519, they left Sanlucar, Spain and headed out into the unknown.

Magellan's five ships sail through stormy weather in this 19th-century book illustration. The members of the expedition had to endure many hardships on the voyage: bad weather, shortages of food and water, disease, and arguments between Magellan and the Spanish ship captains.

The Voyage of a Lifetime

THE VOYAGE set sail with five ships: the *Conceptión*, *San Antonio*, *Santiago*, *Trinidad*, and *Victoria*. Magellan was captain of the *Trinidad*. Juan Serrão, who was the brother of Magellan's good friend Francisco Serrão, was the captain of the *Santiago*. The other three captains were Spanish. These men resented the fact that a Portuguese man was giving them orders.

The ships sailed west for a few weeks, then turned south and crossed the equator. They were on the lookout for Portuguese ships. King Manuel had sent Portuguese warships to intercept Magellan and disrupt his mission, but the Portuguese never found the small Spanish fleet.

The crew sailed along the coast of South America for a few weeks. They stopped for supplies in what is now Rio de Janeiro, Brazil. There, Magellan **converted** some of the natives to Christianity.

In January, they reached Rio de la Plata. This was where Magellan thought the passage was. The crews searched for three weeks, but found no passage. They continued their journey south, following the South American coastline.

The farther south they went, the colder the winds and water got. The crew saw penguins and seals for the first time and called them "geese and sea wolves." Storms were a regular occurrence in these southern waters. Still unable to find the passage through South America, Magellan decided to stop and build winter quarters. They named their landing place Port San Julián for the winter. It was farther south along the coast of South America than any European sailors had ever been.

Magellan said he would be willing to sail as far south as he needed to find the passage through the continent. He didn't believe that South America stretched all the way to the South Pole.

Some of the men were unhappy. Magellan had reduced their daily **ration** of food and water, so that there would be enough for the winter. Some of the Spanish captains made plans to **mutiny** against their leader. Gaspar de

Von Erfindung derselben durch underschiedliche Schiffart. 425

fein kleine Portion / für groß Geld verkauffte/vnnd darnach ihren hungerigen Magen mit rothen Muscheln/ Wurtzeln/Kraut vnd was sie funden fülleten/ darauß endlich ein solche Wassersucht entstanden/ daß ihrer viel mit gesundem Hertzen sterben mussten / wie groß Auffsicht aber die Obersten auff die Essenspeiß hatten/wurden doch zween auff dem Jagschiff den 22. Aprilis zum Strang verurtheilt/weil sie bey Nacht die Speißkammer auffgebrochen/ vnd Oel darauß genommen hatten/der eine ward deß andern Tags auff dem Land an ein Galgen gehenckt/ der ander aber / mit noch einem andern/ so davon gessen/vnd aber nicht angezeigt hatte /zur Geißlung erbetten.

Den 28. Aprilis starb Hauptman Bockholt an der Schwindsucht/nach dem er auff der gantzen Reise fast nie keinen gesundten Tag gehabt/vnd ward auff dem Land Ehrlich begraben/vnd auff jedem Schiff mit dreyen Schüssen zum Grab beleutet. Vnnd folgends mit gemeiner Stimm Sr. Balthasar de Cordes an seine statt verordnet. Darauff er sich ein Hauptman den 3. Maij / auff dem Schiff die Trewe eingestellet. In diesem Hafen starb auch Johannes Corput der Fenderich/auff dem Admiral Schiff/ vnd ward gleicher massen ehrlich begraben.   Den 5. Maij hernach/ ward die Ordnung deß Brodts vermehret/ vnd einem jeden täglich ein halb Pf. Brod gegeben.

Den 7. Maij fuhr der Admiral mit zweyen Nachen nach einer Insel ins Suden/ gerad gegen dem grünen Hafen herüber gelegen/ daselbst Seerobben zusuchen/ vnd als sie dahin kam/ funden sie sieben Nachen mit Wilden Leuthen/ so in die eylff Schuch lang waren / von Farben Whilich/ mit einem langen Haar auff dem Haupt/ da diese der Holländer Nachen gewahr worden/ begaben sie sich mit grosser Eyl zu Land/ vnd begunten so gewaltig mit Steinen zuwerffen/daß sich der Wald-miral nicht zu der Insel nahen dorffte/derhalben/ als die Wilden sahen/ daß sich die Holländer nicht zu Land begeben wolten/ tratten sie mit geschwinder Eyle alle zugleich in ihre Nachen/ vnnd ruderten mit grossem Geschrey an die Holländer/ vnd fiengen zu streiten an/ darauff befahl der Vice-Admiral den Soldaten auff sie loß zubrennen/welches also geschehen/daß ihrer in die fünff auff dem Plaz todt blieben/ dardurch dann solcher schrecken in sie kam/daß sie alsbald wider zu Land eyleten/vñ die Fluche nahmen/ da sie dann etliche Bäume/ so von ferne wol einer Spannen dick sein scheineten/auß der Erden rissen/sich damit zuverschantzen/machten sich auch wider mit Steinen vnd anderm / zuwehren gefast /aber der Vice Admiral verließ solche wütende vnd blutgierige Leute/vnd fuhr vnverrichter Sachen widerumb zu den Schiffen.

Nn iij   Nach

Margin notes:
Sterben viel an der Wassersucht.

z. Soldaten zum Strang verurtheilt.

Hauptman Bockholt stirbt an der Schwindsucht.

5. Nachen mit Wilden den.

This drawing from a 16th-century German book about Magellan's voyage shows the explorer receiving a hostile reception from the natives of South America.

Quesada, the captain of the *Conceptión*, was the leader of the mutiny. Also on his side were Juan de Cartagena, who had been captain of the *San Antonio* before being relieved by Magellan for questioning orders, and Luis de Mendoza, the captain of the *Victoria*.

On April 2, the mutineers seized control of the three ships and demanded that Magellan take them home. In the struggle aboard the *San Antonio*, an unarmed man was killed and captain Alvaro de Mesquita, Magellan's cousin, was captured. Juan de Cartagena once again took over control of the ship.

The Spanish captains wanted to go home. They did not trust Magellan. Not all of the crewmembers wanted to disobey Magellan, however. Captain Juan Serrão of the *Santiago* and his crew remained loyal. So did Magellan's own crew on the *Trinidad*.

Ferdinand Magellan was a determined man. He hadn't come this far just to turn around and go home. He sent a message to the rebel captain of the *Victoria*, Luis de Mendoza. Magellan asked Mendoza if they couldn't talk about what the men wanted. At the same time, Magellan sent another boat, this one filled with armed men. They stormed aboard the *Victoria*, killed Mendoza, and regained control of the ship for Magellan. Magellan then maneuvered his ships so that the two remaining rebel ships could

Antonio Pigafetta

Much of what we know about Magellan's voyage comes from the writings of Antonio Pigafetta, an Italian who volunteered to sail with Ferdinand Magellan. He served his captain-general loyally through the mutiny, as well as the months of sailing into the unknown that followed.

Unknown even to Magellan, Pigafetta kept a diary of the voyage. This diary has provided much information about the voyage and the peoples and customs the European sailors observed during their voyage around the world.

Some of the information is questionable, however. For instance, Pigafetta described the people of Patagonia, in South America, as "giants." However, his descriptions of the geography of the islands that Magellan visited later in his journey, such as Brunei and Cebu, are accurate. His accounts of people of these islands and their cultures were also helpful in expanding Europeans' knowledge of the East.

not escape from the narrow port. After the *Victoria* was recaptured, some of the crews on the other two ships lost their nerve. Cartagena and Quesada had no choice but to surrender.

In all, only 40 of the men had wanted to mutiny. At their trial in Port San Julián, Gaspar de Quesada was sen-

Juan de Cartagena

Juan de Cartagena had years of experience sailing a ship. He had been a captain in Spain's navy. As a loyal Spaniard, he expected to be put in charge of a large voyage. When Ferdinand Magellan, a Portuguese, was named captain-general of the great Spanish voyage to find the sea route through South America, Cartagena was angry and jealous. He agreed to serve as captain of one of the ships, but he also made up his mind to get even.

At one point during the voyage, Cartagena demanded to know why Magellan was following the coast of Africa south, instead of sailing directly southwest across the Atlantic to South America. Magellan told Cartagena to keep his mouth shut and follow orders. When Cartagena challenged Magellan again, Magellan had him arrested and demoted him from command of the *San Antonio*.

Cartagena and those loyal to him made a secret plan to take over the voyage. When the ships were stopped in Port San Julián for the winter, they rebelled. Cartagena helped lead the mutiny.

When Magellan put down the mutiny, he was able to forgive 37 of the 40 men who took part. Cartagena was one of the three who were punished. He and another man was left behind, with a small amount of food and water, in Patagonia when the ships sailed off, and was never heard from again.

tenced to be hanged. Cartagena and the other rebels were chained and put to work pulling the heavy wooden ships out of the water onto the shore. Then they smeared hot tar over the ships so that they would not leak when the journey continued.

Juan de Cartagena, the captain of the *San Antonio*, was sentenced to be *marooned* with another mutineer when the voyage resumed. Magellan *pardoned* the rest of the 40 men, but these men were kept as prisoners and did most of the chores during the ships' stay in Port San Julián. They repaired the ships, cut firewood, and built huts onshore. Magellan's loyal men kept a close eye on the prisoners, but none of them tried to escape.

Among the men who turned against Magellan in the mutiny was Juan Sebastian de Elcano, the navigator of the *Victoria*. Elcano did not share the fate of the other leaders of the mutiny, however. Magellan kept him on the *Victoria* because he needed his experience. In 1522, Elcano would bring the *Victoria* back to Spain with the voyage's survivors.

Magellan and a small group of Portuguese soldiers are attacked by natives of the island of Mactan. Magellan had accomplished his goal of reaching the East Indies by sailing west. He made his greatest mistake of the voyage when he became involved in a dispute between two island chieftains. The error would be fatal.

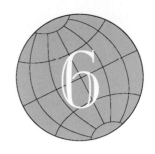

Matters of Life and Death

MAGELLAN HAD MADE up his mind to keep going. In May of 1520, just a month after the mutiny, he sent one of his ships ahead to explore. It was the *Santiago*, captained by Juan Serrão. The *Santiago* sailed farther south and reached the Santa Cruz River. There, a fierce storm knocked the ship ashore. All but one of the 37 men onboard made it ashore, and they watched helplessly as their ship was torn apart by winds and rocks. They carried what they could *salvage* ashore. Then, they sent a group of men back toward Port San Julián where Magellan waited. It took them several days to travel the 60 miles overland, but they made it. Magellan immediately sent a ship with food and supplies to

41

Magellan and his men carefully chart the passage between the Atlantic and Pacific in the illustration above. Sailors later in the century would sail farther south than Magellan had and find Cape Horn, the southernmost tip of South America. Shallows and tricky currents make the strait of Magellan a dangerous sea passage even today. The drawing on the opposite page is from a Dutch book about Magellan's voyage. The sailor greeting natives at the lower right is wearing typical Dutch clothes of the late 16th century.

the stranded men. Miraculously, none of the men had died. They all climbed aboard the rescue ship and returned to Port San Julián. Once they had found berths on the four remaining ships, the voyage continued.

The winds were still cold and the food was still running short, but Magellan was convinced that he would find the strait soon. The ships sailed farther and farther south. Finally, at 52 degrees south, they found what turned out to be the strait. It looked cold and stormy, and even Magellan wasn't sure it was the way to go. Antonio Pigafetta, a man who served with Magellan, wrote in his diary: "We all believed that it was a blind alley."

Magellan sent two ships, the *San Antonio* and the *Conceptión*, ahead to explore. They returned soon after and said the waterway just kept going. All four ships sailed through the strait. The sailing was difficult. Storms swept across the water, moving from coast to coast. At times, the waterway split into two, and both paths would have to be explored. Magellan eventually decided to split his fleet, taking the *Trinidad* and the *Victoria* one way while sending the other two ships in a different direction. When Magellan heard the sound of cannon booming, he turned and sailed back toward the *San Antonio* and *Conceptión*. They had found the route to the Pacific Ocean.

That night, however, the crew of the *San Antonio* decided to return home. They overpowered the captain,

Alvero de Mesquita, and turned the ship for Spain. When Magellan awoke, the *San Antonio* was gone.

Many of the men who remained were afraid that they would never see their homes again. They kept asking Magellan to turn back, but they also respected their leader. When he told them that he wanted to keep going, they agreed to go with him. The three remaining ships set out across the South Sea. Magellan renamed it the Pacific Ocean because it seemed so calm. (Pacific means "peaceful.") Magellan was full of confidence now. He had found the strait he had always believed was there. He had survived several storms and a mutiny. He had saved the crew of one of his ships from certain disaster after that ship had run aground. He also had a map that showed the Spice Islands to be not far away.

Nobody knew how vast the Pacific Ocean was. Nobody had sailed across it before. Magellan thought it was not nearly as wide as the Atlantic and he expected to see his friend Francisco Serrão in less than a week. However, two months later the ships were still sailing.

Among the many things the crew discovered was Tierra del Fuego, or "Land of Fire." This land was to the south of the Strait of Magellan, at the tip of South America. Magellan named it that because he saw many campfires on it as his ships passed.

Magellan kept heading west, but he also headed north slightly, to take advantage of the winds. He was unlucky in that he sailed within a hundred miles or so of several large islands, including Australia and New Zealand, but did not see them. Magellan and his men could have found food and water on these large islands. Although the ships did land at a few small islands, none of them were inhabited or had much food on them. Magellan had to keep going into the open sea. For three months, Magellan and his crew were forced to live on the food and water they had brought with them. The biscuits turned to powder, and the water became stagnant and smelly. Both soon

> **Magellan is said to have told his crew: "Though we have nothing to eat but the leather wrapping from our masts, we shall go on!"**

ran out. The men survived by eating rats and leather and drinking rainwater. Magellan soon discovered that the Portuguese effort to *sabotage* his voyage had succeeded. His records of how much food his ships were carrying had been changed. Only half of the food he thought was onboard was really there.

Magellan refused to turn back. Even though the ships were in the middle of unknown waters, he was convinced that their destination was just ahead. He had no way of knowing how far away they still were. Behind them, however, was only open water. Starving and exhausted, they had no choice but to keep going.

After 98 days of sailing through the Pacific Ocean, Magellan's ships reached Guam, where they stayed for many days. Finally, the sailors could eat good food and drink good water. They were able to rest and recover their strength. They also repaired the ships. Magellan asked the people in Guam about the Spice Islands. The people told him the islands were not far. So the ships headed west again.

They soon came to a group of islands that Europeans had not yet visited. Magellan had never seen so many islands this close together before. The ships stopped off the shore of Cebu, and natives of that island came out to greet the visitors. They had several conversations, and Magellan finally agreed to meet the island king, Datu Humabon.

Cebu and the other islands Magellan visited near the end of his voyage were part of the Philippines, a collection of some 1,600 islands in the South Pacific. These islands were eventually named for King Charles's son Philip.

Magellan's slave, Enrique, proved to be valuable. He was from Malaysia originally, and he found that his language was close to the one spoken by the people of Cebu.

The Spanish told the people of Cebu of the wonders of Europe. They told them of King Charles of Spain, who claimed all the surrounding islands for Spain. They also talked about the Christian religion.

Christians in the 16th century believed it was their duty to convert others to their religion. Magellan had converted some of the native people in Brazil on the first part of the voyage. He wanted to convert more.

Magellan and the other Europeans spoke so convincingly of their religion that the king of Cebu and most of his people converted almost immediately. They wanted to know all about this religion. The Europeans were happy to tell them and were eager to convert people living on nearby islands as well.

Magellan helped further his religious cause by healing a sick man. The man was dying, and the native doctors couldn't help him. Magellan baptized him, proclaimed him a Christian, and the man got up and walked away. The natives were stunned, and even more agreed to become Christians. In two weeks, 2,200 natives of Cebu had converted to Christianity.

At first, Magellan told the natives they could keep their original **idols** and other symbols of worship as long as they believed in Christianity. However, he soon changed his mind. He ordered the native people to convert to Christianity completely or face violence. He also ordered the ones who had converted to burn all the symbols of their

Magellan fights for his life on the beach at Mactan. The commander fought to cover the retreat of his men, who were greatly outnumbered by the hostile natives. Strangely enough, the men who remained on Magellan's ships did not send reinforcements to help him. Magellan was wounded in the arm and leg. The last thing that Antonio Pigafetta saw before escaping the battlefield was Magellan's body floating in the shallow water.

old religion. When one group of people on a neighboring island refused to burn their idols, Magellan ordered their village burned to the ground. What had begun as a peaceful trade mission had turned into a religious crusade.

When Magellan and his group got to the island of Mactan, they found more trouble. One of the local chieftains agreed to see the Europeans and hear about their religion. The other chieftain, a man named Lapulapu, didn't agree. He said his people were doing just fine. He said he was chieftain of his own people and he wouldn't take orders from Datu Humabon or from any other king or chieftain. He also said that he wouldn't welcome Magellan and his crew at all.

Magellan had promised Humabon that if he converted to Christianity, he would be in charge of all the nearby islands. So people from Cebu joined Magellan when he announced that he would attack the people of Mactan. Magellan decided to go ashore himself with 60 of his men. He wanted to show these people how well European soldiers fought.

Magellan's men sailed in a small boat until it stopped on a reef a few yards from the shore. The heavily armored men had to wade through waist-deep water all the way to the shore. When they got there, they found that the natives of Mactan had retreated inland. Magellan's already-tired troops had to march even farther before they got to the enemy. Most of Magellan's men had little fighting experience. When the natives charged, most of the volunteers panicked and ran back toward the shore. Magellan was left alone. He and a handful of men were left to fight about 1,000 natives.

Magellan was killed, and only a few of the 60 men who fought with him returned to the ships. The voyage was suddenly without a leader.

A painting of Magellan holding a sea chart. Although he did not survive the first voyage around the world, Magellan's determination made the trip possible. Other captains might have turned back without accomplishing their goal.

The Homeward Journey

WITH MAGELLAN DEAD, the heart went out of the mission. The remaining sailors got together and elected two leaders: Juan Serrão and Duarte Barbosa. Both had been loyal to Magellan. Barbosa, the son of Magellan's **patron** Diogo Barbosa, had led the soldiers who recaptured the *Victoria* during the mutiny. He took over as captain of the *Trinidad*. He also assumed ownership of Magellan's slave, Enrique. In his will, Magellan had given Enrique his freedom, but Barbosa ignored this fact. He cruelly ordered Enrique to continue serving as a slave to the *Trinidad's* captain—Barbosa himself. He even threatened to make Enrique a slave of Magellan's wife when the voyage returned to Spain. Enrique was angry about his treatment and was determined to get even.

Because Enrique spoke the Malay language, he was able to communicate with the people of Cebu. Enrique went ashore one day and convinced King Humabon that the European sailors were evil and not to be trusted. The king was suspicious of the rest of the sailors, and he had seen that Magellan was not invincible. Also, the sailors had treated the people of Cebu cruelly. The king and Enrique agreed to set a trap.

The king invited 29 sailors, including the captains of the remaining three ships, to a feast on Cebu. The other sailors remained onboard the ships. At the feast, the natives killed the sailors. Enrique disappeared. The people of Cebu tried to get the rest of the sailors to come ashore, but the ships shoved off.

Only 115 men remained. They set out west, hoping to find the Spice Islands. One of the ships, the *Conceptión*, was too damaged to continue. The crew loaded its supplies onto the other two ships and set the

Antonio Pigafetta had been at Magellan's side when he died. He escaped the brutal plot that killed three of the captains on Cebu only because he was still wounded from the battle on Mactan and did not go ashore. He eventually returned to Spain on the *Victoria*.

Juan Sebastian de Elcano

Juan Sebastian de Elcano was born in Spain and lived the life of a sailor from a young age. He had sailed to ports in France and Italy and was an experienced sailor by the time he signed up to sail with Ferdinand Magellan.

He served as ship's master (or second in charge) on the *Conceptión*, one of the five ships on Magellan's voyage. When Juan de Cartagena led the mutiny in Port San Julián on April 2, 1520, Elcano took part. He helped take control of the *Conceptión*. For this, he was given command of the *San Antonio*, which had also rebelled against Magellan.

When Magellan and those men loyal to him had put down the mutiny, Magellan pardoned all but three of the 40 men who had rebelled. Elcano was pardoned and given his job back aboard the *Conceptión*.

He served loyally aboard that ship until it was burned in the Spice Islands in 1521. Later, he assumed command of the *Victoria*. Under Elcano's leadership, the *Victoria* became the only ship from Magellan's voyage to make it home to Spain. Elcano was considered a hero for the rest of his life.

Conceptión on fire. Only the *Victoria* and the *Trinidad* remained. The men did not quite know what to do. Their leader was dead. They were hungry and thirsty. Their ships

A colored woodcut of the *Victoria*, the only one of Magellan's ships to return to Spain. It arrived in 1522, three years after his fleet of five ships had set out. Of the approximately 280 men who set out with Magellan, only 18 survived the journey around the world.

were in bad shape. They didn't really know where the Spice Islands were. They decided to become pirates, seizing money and cargo from other ships they met. They wandered around the unexplored waters, not knowing where to go. They even turned back east for a while and ended up back in the Philippines—only this time, they stayed away from Cebu.

They finally reached the Spice Islands on November 6, 1521. They found that Francisco Serrão, whom Magellan wanted to visit, had died. The Spanish sailors landed on the island of Tidore and made a friend of the *sultan* there. This leader was happy to be a friend of Spain because his enemy, the sultan of Ternate, was a friend of Portugal. Unbelievably, the rivalry between Spain and Portugal stretched halfway across the world!

The east winds were blowing hard by now, and the ships would have to sail soon before the winds changed. *Monsoon* season would make it almost impossible to sail through the Indian Ocean, and the sailors wanted to get through the ocean before the storms began. When it came time to shove off, however, they discovered that the *Trinidad* had sprung a leak. It would take time to repair the ship. They decided that the *Victoria* would shove off anyway to take advantage of the good winds. The ship, carrying 47 men, would sail west around Africa, then north to Spain. The *Trinidad*, meanwhile, would stay behind with 54 men. When they were done repairing the ship, the *Trinidad* would sail back the way they had come, pass through the strait again, and head east across the Atlantic for home. The plan was for both ships to meet in Spain.

It could be argued that Magellan succeeded in sailing around the world. He died in the Philippines, but his voyages as a young man had taken him very near there. Add these to his most famous voyage, and he had sailed around the world.

As had been the case so many times during this voyage, this plan did not work out. The *Trinidad* was blown off course. It ended up getting captured by Portuguese ships. The men on board were thrown in prison, but were eventually allowed to return to Spain.

The *Victoria* sailed onward. A man named Juan Sebastian de Elcano, who had served aboard the *Conceptión*, was elected captain. They sailed the thousands of miles westward in familiar waters. They sailed across the Indian Ocean, around the tip of Africa, and back home. Along the way, they ran out of food and water. Scurvy killed more sailors, and the survivors lived in fear of being overtaken by jealous Portuguese. Still, the leaky ship and its exhausted crew sailed on, returning to Spain on September 8, 1522. Five ships and a crew of about 280 had left Spain three years before. One ship and a crew of 18 had returned. Yet the voyage was considered a success. Magellan was not there to see it, but his idea proved to be the right one. The voyage did indeed reach the Spice Islands by sailing west. It also sent mapmakers scurrying back to their drawing boards.

Both Spain and Portugal now claim success for this first voyage— Portugal because Magellan was Portuguese, and Spain because Magellan sailed under the Spanish flag.

Juan Sebastian de Elcano, the captain of the *Victoria*, was given money and fame. This is a little surprising, because Elcano was one of the men who had turned against Magellan in the mutiny at Port San Julián. The rest of the voyage, however, he was a loyal sailor. He sailed his ship home from the East and lived out his life as a hero.

The voyage of Ferdinand Magellan was important in the history of navigation and science. It proved that the ships of that day could survive extremely long voyages if they were properly equipped. It proved that European settlers had a lot to learn about how to deal with natives of faraway lands. The voyage also proved that the Pacific Ocean was larger than anyone had thought possible. Most of all, however, Magellan's voyage proved that the world was round.

Chronology

1480 Ferdinand Magellan is born in Porto, Portugal.

1488 Bartolomeu Dias becomes the first European to sail around the Cape of Good Hope.

1492 Christopher Columbus reaches the New World.

1493 Pope Alexander VI draws the Line of Demarcation, giving half of the unexplored lands to Spain and half to Portugal.

1498 Vasco da Gama becomes the first European sailor to reach India by sailing around Africa.

1505 Magellan sails with Francisco de Almeida on voyage to India.

1511 Magellan takes part in an expedition to Malacca; when he returns to Portugal, he finds he is out of favor with King Manuel.

1512 Magellan returns to the East, and is wounded in Morocco.

1513 Vasco Núñez de Balboa sees the Pacific Ocean and claims it for Spain.

1515 King Manuel of Portugal refuses Magellan's request for an increase in pay and dismisses him from service.

1517 Magellan leaves Portugal for Spain.

1518 On March 22, Charles V, the king of Spain, grants Magellan money and permission to make a westward voyage to the Spice Islands.

Chronology

1519   In August, Magellan's five ships leave Spain; the ships
        cross the equator November 20; on December 6, the ships
        see Brazil, and a week later they anchor off what is now
        Rio de Janeiro.

1520   On January 10, the ships reach Rio de Plata, which
        Magellan incorrectly believes is the passage to the Pacific;
        on March 31, Magellan announces the ships will spend
        the winter in Port San Julián; a mutiny is put down by
        Magellan and loyal crewmen on April 1; The search for
        the passage resumes in August; on October 21, the ships
        reach the opening of the strait, which they negotiate by
        December.

1521   After a horrible 98-day voyage across the Pacific,
        Magellan's four remaining ships reach Guam in March; On
        March 16, the Philippines are spotted; the crew goes
        ashore on the island of Cebu on April 7; in a battle on the
        island of Mactan, Magellan is killed by hostile natives; the
        remaining ships reach the Moluccas (Spice Islands) on
        November 8; the Trinidad is captured by Portuguese ships.

1522   On September 8, the *Victoria* returns to Spain after sailing
        around the world. Of the 280 men that set out on the
        voyage, 18 are still alive.

Glossary

celestial navigation—a method of steering a ship by observing the positions of the stars.

convert—to bring a person over from one religious view to another.

desert—to leave or run away from a military post without permission, and without intending to return.

idol—a representation or symbol of an object of worship.

isthmus—a narrow strip of land that joins two larger areas of land.

maroon—to put someone ashore on a desolate island and leave him or her to fate.

monsoon—a periodic strong wind with heavy rainfall, usually seasonal.

mutiny—a revolt (usually by a naval crew) against a superior officer.

pardon—an official release from punishment for someone who had committed a crime.

patron—somebody who gives money or other support to another person.

ration—a food allowance for one day.

Glossary

sabotage—to do something that blocks or destroys an effort or goal.

salvage—to rescue or save from wreckage.

scurvy—a disease caused by a lack of vitamin C. Symptoms include loose teeth, bleeding gums, soreness in arm and leg joints, and bleeding into the skin and mucous membranes. Scurvy was common on long sea voyages because of the lack of fresh food and water available.

spices—any of various aromatic plant substances, such as pepper or nutmeg, used to season or flavor foods. These were rare in Europe during the 15th and 16th centuries, and thus were very valuable.

strait—a narrow sea passageway connecting two bodies of water.

sultan—a king or sovereign.

Further Reading

Gallagher, Jim. *Ferdinand Magellan and the First Voyage Around the World.*
Philadelphia: Chelsea House Publishers, 2000.

Hynson, Colin. *Magellan and the Exploration of South America.*
Hauppauge, N.Y.: Barrons Juveniles, 1998.

MacDonald, Fiona. *Magellan: A Voyage Around the World.* Danbury,
Conn.: Franklin Watts, 1998.

McKain, Mark. *The Spanish Exploration of South America.* Philadelphia:
Mason Crest Publishers, 2003.

Pigafetta, Antonio. *The First Voyage Around the World.* New York: Dover,
1994.

Rutsala, David. *The Sea Route to Asia.* Philadelphia: Mason Crest
Publishers, 2003.

Internet Resources

Information about the first voyage around the world
http://www.fordham.edu/halsall/mod/1519magellan.html
http://www.acs.ucalgary.ca/HIST/tutor/eurvoya/index.html

Ferdinand Magellan
http://www.newadvent.org/cathen/09526b.htm
http://marauder.millersv.edu/~columbus/data/art/SCHUES01.ART
http://www.mariner.org/age/magellan.html

Index

Photo Credits

About the Author

David White is the author of several children's books and the author of several history-related Web sites. A former newspaper reporter, editor, and designer, he is now an education professional living in Seaside, California.